Dare the School Build a New Social Order?

George S. Counts

With a New Preface by Wayne J. Urban

Southern Illinois University Press

CARBONDALE AND EDWARDSVILLE

Feffer & Simons, Inc.

LONDON AND AMSTERDAM

Library of Congress Cataloging in Publication Data
Counts, George Sylvester, 1889–1974.
 Dare the school build a new social order?

 (Arcturus books; 143)
 1. Education—Aims and objectives. 2. Education—
United States. 3. Educational sociology—United States.
I. Title.
LC191.C6 1978   301.5'6'0973   78-18895
ISBN 0-8093-0878-9

Preface by Wayne J. Urban copyright © 1978 by Southern
Illinois University Press

06 05 04 03   14 13 12 11

Printed in the United States of America

Preface

GEORGE COUNTS was a major figure in American education for almost fifty years, from the time of his early publications in the 1920s until his death in 1974. Though he was a noted scholar and teacher, this republication of *Dare the School Build a New Social Order?* draws special attention to still another side of Counts's career, his role as a social and political activist. The three parts of *Dare the School* were given originally as speeches in which Counts tried to alert educators to the crisis and challenge of the economic depression of the 1930s and, more importantly, attempted to sketch an educational and political response to that calamity.

Given these circumstances, the urgency and boldness of Counts's words should not be surprising. The following is an example of those qualities:

We can view a world order rushing toward collapse with no more concern than the outcome of a horse race; we can see injustice, crime and misery in their most terrible forms all about us and, if we are not directly affected, register the emotions of a scientist studying white rats in a laboratory. . . . In my opinion, this is a confession of complete moral and spiritual bankruptcy.

Imagine the electrification that these words sure-ly caused in an audience that was probably ex-pecting a dispassionate scholarly address or a speech loaded with platitudes. In contrast with the even tone of most contemporary educational writing and speaking, Counts's call for action was unusually vigorous, even in a time that obviously called for boldness. The effect of Counts's words is demonstrated by the way one group of listen-ers—the Progressive Education Association—re-sponded: they suspended the remainder of the business of the convention in order instead to ponder and react to Counts's ideas.

Another quality that permeates *Dare the School* is its optimism. Despite the crisis, Counts be-lieved that the depression provided an opportu-nity to implement educational and socio econom-ic change in America. This optimism had its roots in Counts's study of American history and his personal experiences as a young boy growing up in rural Kansas. A country which had used the crises of the late 1700s to democratize its political life was capable equally of using the economic depression of the 1930s to extend democrati-zation throughout its social and economic life. America could meet the crisis of the depression in the same way the midwestern farmer handled the challenges of nature, by shrewd planning and hard work. And the school should show the way.

Yet for all his boldness and optimism, Counts's views were not naïve. He earlier had laid the groundwork for the ideas expressed in *Dare the School* through several careful studies of American education. In *The Selective Character of American Secondary Education* (1922), he documented the failure of the public high school to reduce significantly the unequal distribution of wealth and privilege in American society; in *The Social Composition of Boards of Education* (1927), he demonstrated that school boards were controlled completely by the upper classes; and in *School and Society in Chicago* (1928), he chronicled the struggle of Chicago's teachers and citizens to free their schools from economic domination by elites. The conclusion of every one of these studies—that the school was one of many American institutions that did not work for the ordinary citizen but functioned instead to maintain class distinctions—served as a beginning for the arguments in *Dare the School*.

Counts's belief in the necessity of economic and educational change was strengthened by his studies of Soviet Russia in the late 1920s and early 1930s. He made several trips to Russia, where he came face to face with an immense and diverse nation that was attempting consciously to democratize its social, cultural, and economic life, assigning to education a crucial role in that process. Although Counts never saw the Russian experience as a panacea for American problems, he did recognize the importance of the social and educational changes engineered by the Soviets and their usefulness as a laboratory for study by those advocating similar changes in other societies.

Counts's reports on Soviet Russia earned him the epithet of "communist" among some Americans, and his advocacy of social change in *Dare the School* furthered that image. Yet, he was not a communist. Though he did believe that communists should be heard and he published articles by communists in his own journal, *The Social Frontier*, Counts himself never joined the Communist party and never endorsed its platform. In the 1930s and 1940s, he led a battle to expel the communists—because of their totalitarianism—from the American Federation of Teachers. What Counts did believe, a view shared by communists and many liberals, was that economic and social circumstances could be changed. The Great Depression provided the impetus for serious efforts to improve those circumstances; Counts's *Dare the School* was the opening salvo in this battle for change.

Three particular themes in *Dare the School* deserve elaboration because of their importance in Counts's plan for change as well as for their continuing contemporary importance. The first of these is found in Counts's criticism of child-centered progressives. He argued that their naïve belief in education free of social content was in fact a subtle but effective assent to the status quo because it ignored the reality that all education by necessity has a social dimension. To ignore this was to serve the interests of existing social elites. Thus, child-centered progressives were not social progressives but unwitting social conservatives who masked their social views with child-centered language. The discussion in *Dare the School* about the nature of the child is directed toward exposing that fact.

Beliefs similar in effect to those of the child-centered progressives continue to permeate education, so that Counts's observations are still meaningful today. Versions of personalistic, humanistic, and/or therapeutic psychology; the recent advocacy of children's rights; the cynical and alienated "do your own thing" residue of the failure of the youth movement in the 1960s—all these run the risk, with child-centeredness, of ignoring the social dimension of life and education. In addition, the repeated and always unfulfilled claims that the school can "solve" this or that social problem—racial and sexual discrimination and vocational preparation come quickly to mind as examples—drive otherwise sensible educators to the seeming haven of a personalism free of the nasty complexities of social problems. The effect of these movements is that advocates of planned educational and social change are on the defensive while glib sellers of liberation and innovation spout their slogans, collect their grant monies, and wonder why others have become cynical about the efficacy of educational reform.

Given the current cynicism about the school as a reform agency, Counts's formulations about education and change are a welcome tonic, for they avoid the useless extremes of claiming either that the school can do everything or nothing at all in reforming society. Counts skillfully navigated a path between those extremes, noting that though the school was not all powerful, neither was it powerless. He thought that the unique power the school possessed was its ability to formulate an ideal of a democratic society, to communicate that ideal to students, and to encourage them to use the ideal as a standard for judging their own and other societies. If Counts's affirmative answer to his own question *Dare the School Build a New Social Order?* seems a romantic ideal it should be noted that this pursuit of an ideal democracy is an appropriate and feasible goal for any educational institution in a society that claims to be democratic.

A second matter of importance is the role Counts assigns to teachers in achieving educational and social reform. Counts wanted organized teachers to implement both educational reform and the democratization of American society. As members of organized labor and other organized reform movements, teachers could take the lead outside the classroom to implement the democratic ideals they developed and taught within the classroom.

The vision of organized teachers sparking the labor movement to democratize American life has been at best only partially fulfilled in the four decades since Counts proclaimed the challenge. Teachers and other workers now are organized in unprecedented numbers, but neither organized teachers nor the labor movement as a whole are unambiguous proponents of democracy. While seeking the perfectly proper goal of improved economic benefits and working conditions, organized labor oftentimes works against policies that favor previously disadvantaged groups but which are seen as a threat to those already employed and represented by the labor organization. Counts's contention that the common origins of teachers would incline them naturally toward the claims of ordinary, economically oppressed Americans has not been fully realized yet. Certain aspects of teachers' origins, as well as their work environments, have made them defensive in the face of claims by the disadvantaged on the schools.

Despite the uneven record of teachers and

labor in social and political matters, particularly in recent years, the overall achievements of the labor movement and the teachers in it, in the realm of increasing political and economic opportunity for the lower classes, is impressive. Teacher and labor pursuit of unemployment benefits, human welfare reform, the civil rights movements, and many other social and political reforms is impressive. Certainly it is superior to the spotty record of teachers and workers in states where they are not organized. Thus, we can say that working to increase teacher organization, and thereby to increase teachers' potential to participate in democratic reform, certainly is as important today as it was in Counts's time. Were he here now, George Counts certainly would be in the forefront of teacher organization activities, as he was during his life.

A final theme that deserves mention is Counts's idea for reform of the American economy. Counts's belief in democratizing the American economy was firmly in the twentieth-century liberal tradition: government regulation in order to insure protection of the public interest. In turn, this was related to another economic idea, namely, that technological progress had eliminated the scarcity of goods, had provided the conditions for material abundance, and had thereby negated private enterprise's arguments for gross inequalities in wealth premised on the assumption of scarcity. In an age of abundance, extreme poverty was unnecessary and cruel. Government's role as an economic regulator was to make certain that extreme inequalities were abolished.

Recent trends in the American economy, particularly in energy and environmental matters, indicate that Counts's expectations for a technologically induced material abundance were overstated. With old energy sources rapidly being depleted and new energy technologies such as solar and nuclear power presenting access and safety problems, Counts's expectations seem out of place. Yet the very dangers and possibilities in the contemporary situation highlight the continuing timeliness of Counts's major economic idea—that of a governmental role in protecting the public interest. Recent energy shortages and environmental disasters have accented the injustice of an economic system that fails to consider the public interest and continues to pursue profit with a public-be-damned attitude. Both the ecology and consumer movements have focussed on the need for protection of national resources and the preservation of the population from unscrupulous business exploitation. Counts's advocacy of a strong governmental role in the economy is certainly as appropriate now as it was in the 1930s.

In fact, taken as a whole, *Dare the School Build a New Social Order?* is as directly related to the educational and social problems of our time as it was to those of the 1930s. This is not to imply that Counts was prophetic in all his ideas, but rather to emphasize that many of his themes and suggestions, with appropriate modifications, still are applicable today because George Counts provided educators in a democracy with a vision and with ideals that endure.

Wayne J. Urban

Georgia State University
Atlanta, Georgia

Dare the School Build
a New Social Order?

1

LIKE ALL simple and unsophisticated peoples we Americans have a sublime faith in education. Faced with any difficult problem of life we set our minds at rest sooner or later by the appeal to the school. We are convinced that education is the one unfailing remedy for every ill to which man is subject, whether it be vice, crime, war, poverty, riches, injustice, racketeering, political corruption, race hatred, class conflict, or just plain original sin. We even speak glibly and often about the general reconstruction of society through the school. We cling to this faith in spite of the fact that the very period in which our troubles have multiplied so rapidly has witnessed an unprecedented expansion of organized education. This would seem to suggest that our schools, instead of directing the course of change, are themselves driven by the very forces that are transforming the rest of the social order.

The bare fact, however, that simple and unsophisticated peoples have unbounded faith in education does not mean that the faith is untenable. History shows that the intuitions of such folk may be nearer the truth than the weighty and carefully reasoned judgments of the learned and the wise. Under certain conditions education may be as beneficent and as powerful as we are wont to think. But if it is to be so, teachers must abandon much of their easy optimism, subject the concept of education to the most rigorous scrutiny, and be prepared to deal much more fundamentally, realistically, and positively with the American social situation than has been their habit in the past. Any individual or group that would aspire to lead society must be ready to pay the costs of leadership: to accept responsibility, to suffer calumny, to surrender security, to risk both reputation and fortune. If this price, or some important part of it, is not being paid, then the chances are that the claim to leadership is fraudulent. Society is never redeemed without effort, struggle, and sacrifice. Authentic leaders are never found breathing that rarefied atmosphere lying above the dust and smoke of battle. With regard to the past we always recognize the truth of this principle, but when we think of our own times we profess the belief that the ancient roles have been reversed and that now prophets of a new age receive their rewards among the living.

That the existing school is leading the way to a better social order is a thesis which few informed persons would care to defend. Except as it is forced to fight for its own life during times of depression, its course is too serene and untroubled. Only in the rarest of instances does it wage war on behalf of principle or ideal. Almost everywhere it is in the grip of conservative forces and is serving the cause of perpetuating ideas and institutions suited to an age that is gone. But there is one movement above the educational horizon which would seem to show promise of genuine and creative leadership. I refer to the Progressive Education movement. Surely in this union of two of the great faiths of the American people, the faith in progress and the faith in education, we have reason to hope for light and guidance. Here is a movement which would seem to be completely devoted to the promotion of social welfare through education.

Even a casual examination of the program and philosophy of the Progressive schools, however, raises many doubts in the mind. To be sure, these schools have a number of large achievements to their credit. They have focused attention squarely upon the child; they have recognized the fundamental importance of the interest of the learner; they have defended the thesis that activity lies at the root of all true education; they have conceived learning in terms of life situations and growth of character; they have championed the rights of the child as a free personality. Most of this is excellent, but in my judgment it is not enough. It constitutes too narrow a conception of the meaning of education; it brings into the picture but one-half of the landscape.

If an educational movement, or any other movement, calls itself progressive, it must have orientation; it must possess direction. The word itself implies moving forward, and moving forward can have little meaning in the absence of clearly defined purposes. We cannot, like Stephen Leacock's horseman, dash off in all directions at once. Nor should we, like our presidential candidates, evade every disturbing issue and be all things to all men. Also we must beware lest we become so devoted to motion that we neglect the question of direction and be entirely satisfied with movement in circles. Here, I think, we find the fundamental weakness, not only of Progressive Education, but also of American education generally. Like a baby shaking a rattle, we seem to be utterly content with action, provided it is sufficiently vigorous and noisy. In the last analysis a very large part of American educational thought, inquiry, and experimentation is much ado about nothing. And, if we are permitted to push the analogy of the rattle a bit further, our consecration to motion is encouraged and supported in order to keep us out of mischief. At least we know that so long as we thus busy ourselves we shall not incur the serious displeasure of our social elders.

The weakness of Progressive Education thus

lies in the fact that it has elaborated no theory of social welfare, unless it be that of anarchy or extreme individualism. In this, of course, it is but reflecting the viewpoint of the members of the liberal-minded upper middle class who send their children to the Progressive schools—persons who are fairly well-off, who have abandoned the faiths of their fathers, who assume an agnostic attitude towards all important questions, who pride themselves on their open-mindedness and tolerance, who favor in a mild sort of way fairly liberal programs of social reconstruction, who are full of good will and humane sentiment, who have vague aspirations for world peace and human brotherhood, who can be counted upon to respond moderately to any appeal made in the name of charity, who are genuinely distressed at the sight of *unwonted* forms of cruelty, misery, and suffering, and who perhaps serve to soften somewhat the bitter clashes of those real forces that govern the world; but who, in spite of all their good qualities, have no deep and abiding loyalties, possess no convictions for which they would sacrifice over-much, would find it hard to live without their customary material comforts, are rather insensitive to the accepted forms of social injustice, are content to play the role of interested spectator in the drama of human history, refuse to see reality in its harsher and more disagreeable forms, rarely move outside the pleasant circles of the class to which they belong, and in the day of severe trial will follow the lead of the most powerful and respectable forces in society and at the same time find good reasons for so doing. These people have shown themselves entirely incapable of dealing with any of the great crises of our time—war, prosperity, or depression. At bottom they are romantic sentimentalists, but with a sharp eye on the main chance. That they can be trusted to write our educational theories and shape our educational programs is highly improbable.

Among the members of this class the number of children is small, the income relatively high, and the economic functions of the home greatly reduced. For these reasons an inordinate emphasis on the child and child interests is entirely welcome to them. They wish to guard their offspring from too strenuous endeavor and from coming into too intimate contact with the grimmer aspects of industrial society. They wish their sons and daughters to succeed according to the standards of their class and to be a credit to their parents. At heart feeling themselves members of a superior human strain, they do not want their children to mix too freely with the children of the poor or of the less fortunate races. Nor do they want them to accept radical social doctrines, espouse unpopular causes, or lose themselves in quest of any Holy Grail. According to their views education should deal with life, but with life at a distance or in a highly diluted form. They would generally maintain that life should be kept at arm's length, if it should not be handled with a poker.

If Progressive Education is to be genuinely progressive, it must emancipate itself from the influence of this class, face squarely and courageously every social issue, come to grips with life in all of its stark reality, establish an organic relation with the community, develop a realistic and comprehensive theory of welfare, fashion a compelling and challenging vision of human destiny, and become less frightened than it is today at the bogies of *imposition* and *indoctrination*. In a word, Progressive Education cannot place its trust in a child-centered school.

This brings us to the most crucial issue in education—the question of the nature and extent of the influence which the school should exercise over the development of the child. The advocates of extreme freedom have been so successful in championing what they call the rights of the child that even the most skillful practitioners of the art of converting others to their opinions disclaim all intention of molding the learner. And when the word indoctrination is coupled with education there is scarcely one among us possessing the hardihood to refuse to be horrified. This feeling is so widespread that even Mr. Luna-

7

charsky, Commissar of Education in the Russian Republic until 1929, assured me on one occasion that the Soviet educational leaders do not believe in the indoctrination of children in the ideas and principles of communism. When I asked him whether their children become good communists while attending the schools, he replied that the great majority do. On seeking from him an explanation of this remarkable phenomenon he said that Soviet teachers merely tell their children the truth about human history. As a consequence, so he asserted, practically all of the more intelligent boys and girls adopt the philosophy of communism. I recall also that the Methodist sect in which I was reared always confined its teachings to the truth!

The issue is no doubt badly confused by historical causes. The champions of freedom are obviously the product of an age that has broken very fundamentally with the past and is equally uncertain about the future. In many cases they feel themselves victims of narrow orthodoxies which were imposed upon them during childhood and which have severely cramped their lives. At any suggestion that the child should be influenced by his elders they therefore envisage the establishment of a state church, the formulation of a body of sacred doctrine, and the teaching of this doctrine as fixed and final. If we are forced to choose between such an unenlightened form of pedagogical influence and a condition of complete freedom for the child, most of us would in all probability choose the latter as the lesser of two evils. But this is to create a wholly artificial situation: the choice should not be limited to these two extremes. Indeed today neither extreme is possible.

I believe firmly that a critical factor must play an important role in any adequate educational program, at least in any such program fashioned for the modern world. An education that does not strive to promote the fullest and most thorough understanding of the world is not worthy of the name. Also there must be no deliberate distortion or suppression of facts to support any theory or point of view. On the other hand, I am prepared to defend the thesis that all education contains a large element of imposition, that in the very nature of the case this is inevitable, that the existence and evolution of society depend upon it, that it is consequently* eminently desirable, and that the frank acceptance of this fact by the educator is a major professional obligation. I even contend that failure to do this involves the clothing of one's own deepest prejudices in the garb of universal truth and the introduction into the theory and practice of education of an element of

---

*Some persons would no doubt regard this as a *non sequitur*, but the great majority of the members of the human race would, I think, accept the argument.

obscurantism. In the development of this thesis I shall examine a number of widespread fallacies which seem to me to underlie the theoretical opposition to all forms of imposition. Although certain of these fallacies are very closely related and to some extent even cover the same territory, their separate treatment will help to illuminate the problem.

2

1. THERE IS the fallacy that man is born free. As a matter of fact, he is born helpless. He achieves freedom, as a race and as an individual, through the medium of culture. The most crucial of all circumstances conditioning human life is birth into a particular culture. By birth one becomes a Chinese, an Englishman, a Hottentot, a Sioux Indian, a Turk, or a one-hundred-percent American. Such a range of possibilities may appear too shocking to contemplate, but it is the price that one must pay in order to be born. Nevertheless, even if a given soul should happen by chance to choose a Hottentot for a mother, it should thank its lucky star that it was born into the Hottentot culture rather than entirely free. By being nurtured on a body of culture, however backward and limited it may be comparatively, the individual is at once imposed upon and liberated. The child is terribly imposed upon by being compelled through the accidents of birth to learn one language rather than another, but without some language man would never become man. Any language, even the most poverty-stricken, is infinitely better than none at all. In the life

cycle of the individual many choices must of necessity be made, and the most fundamental and decisive of these choices will always be made by the group. This is so obvious that it should require no elaboration. Yet this very obvious fact, with its implications, is commonly disregarded by those who are fearful of molding the child.

One of the most important elements of any culture is a tradition of achievement along a particular line—a tradition which the group imposes upon the young and through which the powers of the young are focused, disciplined, and developed. One people will have a fine hunting tradition, another a maritime tradition, another a musical tradition, another a military tradition, another a scientific tradition, another a baseball tradition, another a business tradition, and another even a tradition of moral and religious prophecy. A particular society of the modern type commonly has a vast number of different traditions all of which may be bound together and integrated more or less by some broad and inclusive tradition. One might argue that the imposing of these traditions upon children involves a severe restriction upon their freedom. My thesis is that such imposition, provided the tradition is vital and suited to the times, releases the energies of the young, sets up standards of excellence, and makes possible really great achievement. The individual who fails to come under the influence of such a tradition may enjoy a certain kind of freedom, but it is scarcely a kind of freedom that anyone would covet for either himself or his children. It is the freedom of mediocrity, incompetence, and aimlessness.

2. There is the fallacy that the child is good by nature. The evidence from anthropology, as well as from common observation, shows that on entering the world the individual is neither good nor bad; he is merely a bundle of potentialities which may be developed in manifold directions. Guidance is, therefore, not to be found in child nature, but rather in the culture of the group and the purposes of living. There can be no good individual apart from some conception of the character of the *good* society; and the good society is not something that is given by nature: it must be fashioned by the hand and brain of man. This process of building a good society is to a very large degree an educational process. The nature of the child must of course be taken into account in the organization of any educational program, but it cannot furnish the materials and the guiding principles of that program. Squirm and wriggle as we may, we must admit that the bringing of materials and guiding principles from the outside involves the molding of the child.

3. There is the fallacy that the child lives in a separate world of his own. The advocates of freedom often speak of the adult as an alien influence

in the life of the child. For an adult to intrude himself or his values into the domain of boys and girls is made to take on the appearance of an invasion by a foreign power. Such a dualism is almost wholly artificial. Whatever may be the view of the adult, the child knows but one society; and that is a society including persons of all ages. This does not mean that conflicts of interest may not occur or that on occasion adults may not abuse and exploit children. It does mean that in a proper kind of society the relationship is one of mutual benefit and regard in which the young repay in trust and emulation the protection and guidance provided by their elders. The child's conception of his position in society is well expressed in the words of Plenty-coups, the famous Crow chieftain, who spoke thus of his boyhood: "We followed the buffalo herds over our beautiful plains, fighting a battle one day and sending out a war-party against the enemy the next. My heart was afire. I wished so to help my people, to distinguish myself, so that I might wear an eagle's feather in my hair. How I worked to make my arms strong as a grizzly's, and how I practiced with my bow! A boy never wished to be a man more than I." Here is an emphatic and unequivocal answer to those who would raise a barrier between youth and age. Place the child in a world of his own and you take from him the most powerful incentives to growth and achievement. Perhaps one of the greatest tragedies of contemporary society lies in the fact that the child is becoming increasingly isolated from the serious activities of adults. Some would say that such isolation is an inevitable corollary of the growing complexity of the social order. In my opinion it is rather the product of a society that is moved by no great commanding ideals and is consequently victimized by the most terrible form of human madness—the struggle for private gain. As primitive peoples wisely protect their children from the dangers of actual warfare, so we guard ours from the acerbities of economic strife. Until school and society are bound together by common purposes the program of education will lack both meaning and vitality.

4. There is the fallacy that education is some pure and mystical essence that remains unchanged from everlasting to everlasting. According to this view, genuine education must be completely divorced from politics, live apart from the play of social forces, and pursue ends peculiar to itself. It thus becomes a method existing independently of the cultural milieu and equally beneficent at all times and in all places. This is one of the most dangerous of fallacies and is responsible for many sins committed in different countries by American educators traveling abroad. They have carried the same brand of education to backward and advanced races, to

peoples living under relatively static conditions and to peoples passing through periods of rapid and fundamental transition. They have called it Education with a capital *E*, whereas in fact it has been American education with a capital *A* and a small *e*. Any defensible educational program must be adjusted to a particular time and place, and the degree and nature of the imposition must vary with the social situation. Under ordinary conditions the process of living suffices in itself to hold society together, but when the forces of disintegration become sufficiently powerful it may well be that a fairly large measure of deliberate control is desirable and even essential to social survival.

5. There is the fallacy that the school should be impartial in its emphases, that no bias should be given instruction. We have already observed how the individual is inevitably molded by the culture into which he is born. In the case of the school a similar process operates and presumably is subject to a degree of conscious direction. My thesis is that complete impartiality is utterly impossible, that the school must shape attitudes, develop tastes, and even impose ideas. It is obvious that the whole of creation cannot be brought into the school. This means that some selection must be made of teachers, curricula, architecture, methods of teaching. And in the making of the selection the dice must always be weighted

in favor of this or that. Here is a fundamental truth that cannot be brushed aside as irrelevant or unimportant; it constitutes the very essence of the matter under discussion. Nor can the reality be concealed beneath agreeable phrases. Professor Dewey states in his *Democracy and Education* that the school should provide a *purified* environment for the child. With this view I would certainly agree; probably no person reared in our society would favor the study of pornography in the schools. I am sure, however, that this means stacking the cards in favor of the particular systems of value which we may happen to possess. It is one of the truisms of the anthropologist that there are no maxims of purity on which all peoples would agree. Other vigorous opponents of imposition unblushingly advocate the "cultivation of democratic sentiments" in children or the promotion of child growth in the direction of "a better and richer life." The first represents definite acquiescence in imposition; the second, if it does not mean the same thing, means nothing. I believe firmly that democratic sentiments should be cultivated and that a better and richer life should be the outcome of education, but in neither case would I place responsibility on either God or the order of nature. I would merely contend that as educators we must make many choices involving the development of attitudes in boys and girls and that we should not be afraid to acknowledge the faith that is in us or mayhap the forces that compel us.

6. There is the fallacy that the great object of education is to produce the college professor, that is, the individual who adopts an agnostic attitude towards every important social issue, who can balance the pros against the cons with the skill of a juggler, who sees all sides of every question and never commits himself to any, who delays action until all the facts are in, who knows that all the facts will never come in, who consequently holds his judgment in a state of indefinite suspension, and who before the approach of middle age sees his powers of action atrophy and his social sympathies decay. With Peer Gynt he can exclaim:

Ay, think of it—wish it done—will it to boot,—
But do it—! No, that's past my understanding!

This type of mind also talks about waiting until the solutions of social problems are found, when as a matter of fact there are no solutions in any definite and final sense. For any complex social problem worthy of the name there are probably tens and even scores, if not hundreds, of "solutions," depending upon the premises from which one works. The meeting of a social situation involves the making of decisions and the working out of adjustments. Also it involves the selection and rejection of values. If we wait for a solution to appear like the bursting of the sun through the clouds or the resolving of the elements in an algebraic equation, we shall wait in vain. Although college professors, if not too numerous, perform a valuable social function, society requires great numbers of persons who, while capable of gathering and digesting facts, are at the same time able to think in terms of life, make decisions, and act. From such persons will come our real social leaders.

7. There is the closely related fallacy that education is primarily intellectualistic in its processes and goals. Quite as important is that ideal factor in culture which gives meaning, direction, and significance to life. I refer to the element of faith or purpose which lifts man out of himself and above the level of his more narrow personal interests. Here, in my judgment, is one of the great lacks in our schools and in our intellectual class today. We are able to contemplate the universe and find that all is vanity. Nothing really stirs us, unless it be that the bath water is cold, the toast burnt, or the elevator not running; or that perchance we miss the first section of a revolving door. Possibly this is the fundamental reason why we are so fearful of molding the child. We are moved by no great faiths; we are touched by no great passions. We can view a world order rushing rapidly towards collapse with no more concern than the outcome of a horse

race; we can see injustice, crime and misery in their most terrible forms all about us and, if we are not directly affected, register the emotions of a scientist studying white rats in a laboratory. And in the name of freedom, objectivity, and the open mind, we would transmit this general attitude of futility to our children. In my opinion this is a confession of complete moral and spiritual bankruptcy. We cannot, by talk about the interests of children and the sacredness of personality, evade the responsibility of bringing to the younger generation a vision which will call forth their active loyalties and challenge them to creative and arduous labors. A generation without such a vision is destined, like ours, to a life of absorption in self, inferiority complexes, and frustration. The genuinely free man is not the person who spends the day contemplating his own navel, but rather the one who loses himself in a great cause or glorious adventure.

8. There is the fallacy that the school is an all-powerful educational agency. Every professional group tends to exaggerate its own importance in the scheme of things. To this general rule the teachers offer no exception. The leaders of Progressive Education in particular seem to have an over-weening faith in the power of the school. On the one hand, they speak continually about reconstructing society through education; and on the other, they apparently live in a state of per-

petual fear lest the school impose some one point of view upon all children and mold them all to a single pattern. A moment's reflection is sufficient to show that life in the modern world is far too complex to permit this: the school is but one formative agency among many, and certainly not the strongest at that. Our major concern consequently should be, not to keep the school from influencing the child in a positive direction, but rather to make certain that every Progressive school will use whatever power it may possess in opposing and checking the forces of social conservatism and reaction. We know full well that, if the school should endeavor vigorously and consistently to win its pupils to the support of a given social program, unless it were supported by other agencies, it could act only as a mild counterpoise to restrain and challenge the might of less enlightened and more selfish purposes.

9. There is the fallacy that ignorance rather than knowledge is the way of wisdom. Many who would agree that imposition of some kind is inevitable seem to feel that there is something essentially profane in any effort to understand, plan, and control the process. They will admit that the child is molded by his environment, and then presumably contend that in the fashioning of this environment we should close our eyes to the consequences of our acts, or at least should not endeavor to control our acts in the light of

definite knowledge of their consequences. To do the latter would involve an effort to influence deliberately the growth of the child in a particular direction—to cause him to form this habit rather than that, to develop one taste rather than another, to be sensitive to a given ideal rather than its rival. But this would be a violation of the "rights of the child," and therefore evil. Apparently his rights can be protected only if our influence upon him is thoroughly concealed under a heavy veil of ignorance. If the school can do no better than this, it has no reason for existence. If it is to be merely an arena for the blind play of psychological forces, it might better close its doors. Here is the doctrine of *laissez faire*, driven from the field of social and political theory, seeking refuge in the domain of pedagogy. Progressive Education wishes to build a new world but refuses to be held accountable for the kind of world it builds. In my judgment, the school should know what it is doing, in so far as this is humanly possible, and accept full responsibility for its acts.

10. Finally, there is the fallacy that in a dynamic society like ours the major responsibility of education is to prepare the individual to adjust himself to social change. The argument in support of this view is fairly cogent. The world is changing with great rapidity; the rate of change is being accelerated constantly; the future is full

of uncertainty. Consequently the individual who is to live and thrive in this world must possess an agile mind, be bound by no deep loyalties, hold all conclusions and values tentatively, and be ready on a moment's notice to make even fundamental shifts in outlook and philosophy. Like a lumberjack riding a raft of logs through the rapids, he must be able with lightning speed to jump from one insecure foundation to another, if he is not to be overwhelmed by the onward surge of the cultural stream. In a word, he must be as willing to adopt new ideas and values as to install the most up-to-the-minute labor saving devices in his dwelling or to introduce the latest inventions into his factory. Under such a conception of life and society, education can only bow down before the gods of chance and reflect the drift of the social order. This conception is essentially anarchic in character, exalts the irrational above the rational forces of society, makes of security an individual rather than a social goal, drives every one of us into an insane competition with his neighbors, and assumes that man is incapable of controlling in the common interest the creatures of his brain. Here we have imposition with a vengeance, but not the imposition of the teacher or the school. Nor is it an enlightened form of imposition. Rather is it the imposition of the chaos and cruelty and ugliness produced by the brutish struggle for existence and advantage. Far more terrifying than any indoctrination in which the school might indulge is the prospect of our becoming completely victimized and molded by the mechanics of industrialism. The control of the machine requires a society which is dominated less by the ideal of individual advancement and more by certain far-reaching purposes and plans for social construction. In such a society, instead of the nimble mind responsive to every eddy in the social current, a firmer and more steadfast mentality would be preferable.

3

IF WE MAY now assume that the child will be imposed upon in some fashion by the various elements in his environment, the real question is not whether imposition will take place, but rather from what source it will come. If we were to answer this question in terms of the past, there could, I think, be but one answer: on all genuinely crucial matters the school follows the wishes of the groups or classes that actually rule society; on minor matters the school is sometimes allowed a certain measure of freedom. But the future may be unlike the past. Or perhaps I should say that teachers, if they could increase sufficiently their stock of courage, intelligence, and vision, might become a social force of some magnitude. About this eventuality I am not over sanguine, but a society lacking leadership as ours does, might even accept the guidance of teachers. Through powerful organizations they might at least reach the public conscience and come to exercise a larger measure of control over the schools than hitherto. They would then have to assume some responsibility for the more fundamental forms of imposition which, according to my argument, cannot be avoided.

That the teachers should deliberately reach for power and then make the most of their conquest is my firm conviction. To the extent that they are permitted to fashion the curriculum and the procedures of the school they will definitely and positively influence the social attitudes, ideals, and behavior of the coming generation. In doing this they should resort to no subterfuge or false modesty. They should say neither that they are merely teaching the truth nor that they are unwilling to wield power in their own right. The first position is false and the second is a confession of incompetence. It is my observation that the men and women who have affected the course of human events are those who have not hesitated to use the power that has come to them. Representing as they do, not the interests of the moment or of any special class, but rather the common and abiding interests of the people, teachers are under heavy social obligation to protect and further those interests. In this they occupy a relatively unique position in society. Also since the profession should embrace scientists and scholars of the highest rank, as well as teachers working at all levels of the educational system, it has at its disposal, as no other group, the knowledge and wisdom of the ages. It is scarcely thinkable that these men and women would ever act as selfishly or bungle as badly as have the so-called "practical" men of our generation—the politicians, the financiers, the industrialists. If all of these facts are taken into account, instead of shunning power, the profession should rather seek power and then strive to use that power fully and wisely and in the interests of the great masses of the people.

The point should be emphasized that teachers possess no magic secret to power. While their work should give them a certain moral advantage, they must expect to encounter the usual obstacles blocking the road to leadership. They should not be deceived by the pious humbug with which public men commonly flatter the members of the profession. To expect ruling groups or classes to give precedence to teachers on important matters, because of age or sex or sentiment, is to refuse to face realities. It was one of the proverbs of the agrarian order that a spring never rises higher than its source. So the power that teachers exercise in the schools can be no greater than the power they wield in society. Moreover, while organization is necessary, teachers should not think of their problem primarily in terms of organizing and presenting a united front to the world, the flesh, and the devil. In order to be effective they must throw off completely the slave psychology that has dominated the mind of the pedagogue more or less since the days of ancient Greece. They must be prepared to stand on their own feet and win for their ideas the support of the masses of the people. Education as a force for social regeneration must march hand in hand with the living and creative forces of the social order. In their own lives teachers must bridge the gap between school and society and play some part in the fashioning of those great common purposes which should bind the two together.

This brings us to the question of the kind of imposition in which teachers should engage, if they had the power. Our obligations, I think, grow out of the social situation. We live in troublous times; we live in an age of profound change; we live in an age of revolution. Indeed it is highly doubtful whether man ever lived in a more eventful period than the present. In order to match our epoch we would probably have to go back to the fall of the ancient empires or even to that unrecorded age when men first abandoned the natural arts of hunting and fishing and trapping and began to experiment with agriculture and the settled life. Today we are witnessing the rise of a civilization quite without precedent in human history—a civilization founded on science, technology, and machinery, possessing the most extraordinary power, and rapidly making of the entire world a single great society. Because of forces already released, whether in the field of economics, politics, morals, religion, or art, the old molds are being broken. And the peoples of the earth are everywhere seething with strange ideas and passions. If life were peaceful and quiet and undisturbed by great issues, we might with some show of wisdom center our attention on the nature of the child. But with the world as it is, we cannot afford for a single instant to remove our eyes from the social scene or shift our attention from the peculiar needs of the age.

In this new world that is forming, there is one set of issues which is peculiarly fundamental and which is certain to be the center of bitter and prolonged struggle. I refer to those issues which may be styled economic. President Butler has well stated the case: "For a generation and more past," he says, "the center of human interest has been moving from the point which it occupied for some four hundred years to a new point which it bids fair to occupy for a time equally long. The shift in the position of the center of gravity in human interest has been from politics to economics; from considerations that had to do with forms of government, with the establishment and protection of individual liberty, to considerations that have to do with the production, distribution, and consumption of wealth."

Consider the present condition of the nation. Who among us, if he had not been reared amid our institutions, could believe his eyes as he surveys the economic situation, or his ears as he listens to solemn disquisitions by our financial and political leaders on the cause and cure of the depression! Here is a society that manifests the most extraordinary contradictions: a mastery over the forces of nature, surpassing the wildest dreams of antiquity, is accompanied by extreme material insecurity; dire poverty walks hand in hand with the most extravagant living the world has ever known; an abundance of goods of all kinds is coupled with privation, misery, and even starvation; an excess of production is seriously offered as the underlying cause of severe physical suffering; breakfastless children march to school past bankrupt shops laden with rich foods gathered from the ends of the earth; strong men by the million walk the streets in a futile search for employment and with the exhaustion of hope enter the ranks of the damned; great captains of industry close factories without warning and dismiss the workmen by whose labors they have amassed huge fortunes through the years; automatic machinery increasingly displaces men and threatens society with a growing contingent of the permanently unemployed; racketeers and gangsters with the connivance of public officials fasten themselves on the channels of trade and exact toll at the end of the machine gun; economic parasitism, either within or without the law, is so prevalent that the tradition of honest labor is showing signs of decay; the wages paid to the workers are too meager to enable them to buy back the goods they produce; consumption is subordinated to production and a philosophy of deliberate waste is widely proclaimed as the highest economic wisdom; the science of psychology is employed to fan the flames of desire so that men may be enslaved by their wants and bound to the wheel of production; a government board advises the cotton-growers to plow under every third row of cotton in order to bolster up the market; both ethical and æsthetic considerations are commonly over-ridden by "hard-headed business men" bent on material gain; federal aid to the unemployed is opposed on the ground that it would pauperize the masses when the favored members of society have always lived on a dole; even responsible leaders resort to the practices of the witch doctor and vie with one another in predicting the return of prosperity; an ideal of rugged individualism, evolved in a simple pioneering and agrarian order at a time when free land existed in abundance, is used to justify a system which exploits pitilessly and without thought of the morrow the natural and human resources of the nation and of the world. One can only imagine what Jeremiah would say if he could step out of the pages of the Old Testament and cast his eyes over this vast spectacle so full of tragedy and of menace.

The point should be emphasized, however, that the present situation is also freighted with hope and promise. The age is pregnant with possibilities. There lies within our grasp the most humane, the most beautiful, the most majestic civilization ever fashioned by any people. This much at least we know today. We shall probably know more tomorrow. At last men have achieved such a mastery over the forces of nature that wage slavery can follow chattel slavery and take its place among the relics of the past. No longer are there grounds for the contention that the finer fruits of human culture must be nurtured upon the toil and watered by the tears of the masses. The limits to achievement set by nature have been so extended that we are today bound merely by our ideals, by our power of self-discipline, by our ability to devise social arrangements suited to an industrial age. If we are to place any credence whatsoever in the word of our engineers, the full utilization of modern technology at its present level of development should enable us to produce several times as much goods as were ever produced at the very peak of prosperity, and with the working day, the working year, and the working life reduced by half. We hold within our hands the power to usher in an age of plenty, to make secure the lives of all, and to banish poverty forever from the land. The only cause for doubt or pessimism lies in the question of our ability to rise to the stature of the times in which we live.

Our generation has the good or the ill fortune to live in an age when great decisions must be made. The American people, like most of the other peoples of the earth, have come to the parting of the ways; they can no longer trust entirely the inspiration which came to them when the Republic was young; they must decide afresh what they are to do with their talents. Favored above all other nations with the resources of nature and the material instrumentalities of civilization, they stand confused and irresolute before the future. They seem to lack the moral quality necessary to quicken, discipline, and give direction to their matchless energies. In a recent paper Professor Dewey has, in my judgment, correctly diagnosed our troubles: "the schools, like the nation," he says, "are in need of a central purpose which will create new enthusiasm and devotion, and which will unify and guide all intellectual plans."

This suggests, as we have already observed, that the educational problem is not wholly intellectual in nature. Our Progressive schools therefore cannot rest content with giving children an opportunity to study contemporary society in all of its aspects. This of course must be done, but

I am convinced that they should go much farther. If the schools are to be really effective, they must become centers for the building, and not merely for the contemplation, of our civilization. This does not mean that we should endeavor to promote particular reforms through the educational system. We should, however, give to our children a vision of the possibilities which lie ahead and endeavor to enlist their loyalties and enthusiasms in the realization of the vision. Also our social institutions and practices, all of them, should be critically examined in the light of such a vision.

4

IN *The Epic of America* James Truslow Adams contends that our chief contribution to the heritage of the race lies not in the field of science, or religion, or literature, or art but rather in the creation of what he calls the "American Dream" —a vision of a society in which the lot of the common man will be made easier and his life enriched and ennobled. If this vision has been a moving force in our history, as I believe it has, why should we not set ourselves the task of revitalizing and reconstituting it? This would seem to be the great need of our age, both in the realm of education and in the sphere of public life, because men must have something for which to live. Agnosticism, skepticism, or even experimentalism, unless the last is made flesh through the formulation of some positive social program, constitutes an extremely meager spiritual diet for any people. A small band of intellectuals, a queer breed of men at best, may be satisfied with such a spare ration, particularly if they lead the sheltered life common to their class; but the masses, I am sure, will always demand something more solid and substantial. Ordinary men and women crave a tangible purpose towards which to strive and which lends richness and dignity and meaning to life. I would consequently like to see our profession come to grips with the problem of creating a tradition that has roots in American soil, is in harmony with the spirit of the age, recognizes the facts of industrialism, appeals to the most profound impulses of our people, and takes into account the emergence of a world society.*

The ideal foundations on which we must build are easily discernible. Until recently the very word America has been synonymous throughout the world with democracy and symbolic to the oppressed classes of all lands of hope and opportunity. Child of the revolutionary ideas and impulses of the eighteenth century, the American nation became the embodiment of bold social experimentation and a champion of the power of environment to develop the capacities and redeem the souls of common men and women. And as her stature grew, her lengthening shadow reached to the four corners of the earth and everywhere impelled the human will to rebel

---

*In the remainder of the argument I confine attention entirely to the domestic situation. I do this, not because I regard the question of international relations unimportant, but rather because of limitations of space. All I can say here is that any proper conception of the world society must accept the principle of the moral equality of races and nations.

against ancient wrongs. Here undoubtedly is the finest jewel in our heritage and the thing that is most worthy of preservation. If America should lose her honest devotion to democracy, or if she should lose her revolutionary temper, she will no longer be America. In that day, if it has not already arrived, her spirit will have fled and she will be known merely as the richest and most powerful of the nations. If America is not to be false to the promise of her youth, she must do more than simply perpetuate the democratic ideal of human relationships: she must make an intelligent and determined effort to fulfill it. The democracy of the past was the chance fruit of a strange conjunction of forces on the new continent; the democracy of the future can only be the intended offspring of the union of human reason, purpose, and will. The conscious and deliberate achievement of democracy under novel circumstances is the task of our generation.

Democracy of course should not be identified with political forms and functions—with the federal constitution, the popular election of officials, or the practice of universal suffrage. To think in such terms is to confuse the entire issue, as it has been confused in the minds of the masses for generations. The most genuine expression of democracy in the United States has little to do with our political institutions: it is a sentiment with respect to the moral equality of men: it is an aspiration towards a society in which this sentiment will find complete fulfillment. A society fashioned in harmony with the American democratic tradition would combat all forces tending to produce social distinctions and classes; repress every form of privilege and economic parasitism; manifest a tender regard for the weak, the ignorant, and the unfortunate; place the heavier and more onerous social burdens on the backs of the strong; glory in every triumph of man in his timeless urge to express himself and to make the world more habitable; exalt human labor of hand and brain as the creator of all wealth and culture; provide adequate material and spiritual rewards for every kind of socially useful work; strive for genuine equality of opportunity among all races, sects, and occupations; regard as paramount the abiding interests of the great masses of the people; direct the powers of government to the elevation and the refinement of the life of the common man; transform or destroy all conventions, institutions, and special groups inimical to the underlying principles of democracy; and finally be prepared as a last resort, in either the defense or the realization of this purpose, to follow the method of revolution. Although these ideals have never been realized or perhaps even fully accepted anywhere in the United States and have always had to struggle for existence with contrary forces, they nevertheless have authentic roots in the past. They are the values for which America has stood before the world during most of her history and with which the American people have loved best to associate their country. Their power and authority are clearly revealed in the fact that selfish interests, when grasping for some special privilege, commonly wheedle and sway the masses by repeating the words and kneeling before the emblems of the democratic heritage.

It is becoming increasingly clear, however, that this tradition, if its spirit is to survive, will have to be reconstituted in the light of the great social trends of the age in which we live. Our democratic heritage was largely a product of the frontier, free land, and a simple agrarian order. Today a new and strange and closely integrated industrial economy is rapidly sweeping over the world. Although some of us in our more sentimental moments talk wistfully of retiring into the more tranquil society of the past, we could scarcely induce many of our fellow citizens to accompany us. Even the most hostile critics of industrialism would like to take with them in their retirement a few such fruits of the machine as electricity, telephones, automobiles, modern plumbing, and various labor-saving devices, or at least be assured of an abundant supply of slaves or docile and inexpensive servants. But all such talk is the most idle chatter. For better or for worse we must take industrial civilization as an enduring fact: already we have become parasitic on its institutions and products. The hands of the clock cannot be turned back.

If we accept industrialism, as we must, we are then compelled to face without equivocation the most profound issue which this new order of society has raised and settle that issue in terms of the genius of our people—the issue of the control of the machine. In whose interests and for what purposes are the vast material riches, the unrivaled industrial equipment, and the science and technology of the nation to be used? In the light of our democratic tradition there can be but one answer to the question: all of these resources must be dedicated to the promotion of the welfare of the great masses of the people. Even the classes in our society that perpetually violate this principle are compelled by the force of public opinion to pay lip-service to it and to defend their actions in its terms. No body of men, however powerful, would dare openly to flout it. Since the opening of the century the great corporations have even found it necessary to establish publicity departments or to employ extremely able men as public relations counselors in order to persuade the populace that regardless of appearances they are lovers of democracy and devoted servants of the people. In this they have been remarkably successful, at least until the coming of the Great Depression. For during the past generation there have been few things in America that could not be bought at a price.

If the benefits of industrialism are to accrue fully to the people, this deception must be exposed. If the machine is to serve all, and serve all equally, it cannot be the property of the few. To ask these few to have regard for the common weal, particularly when under the competitive system they are forced always to think first of themselves or perish, is to put too great a strain on human nature. With the present concentration of economic power in the hands of a small class, a condition that is likely to get worse before it gets better, the survival or development of a society that could in any sense be called democratic is unthinkable. The hypocrisy which is so characteristic of our public life today is due primarily to our failure to acknowledge the fairly obvious fact that America is the scene of an irreconcilable conflict between two opposing forces. On the one side is the democratic tradition inherited from the past; on the other is a system of economic arrangements which increasingly partakes of the nature of industrial feudalism. Both of these forces cannot survive: one or the other must give way. Unless the democratic tradition is able to organize and conduct a successful attack on the economic system, its complete destruction is inevitable.

If democracy is to survive, it must seek a new economic foundation. Our traditional democracy rested upon small-scale production in both agriculture and industry and a rather general diffusion of the rights of property in capital and natural resources. The driving force at the root of this condition, as we have seen, was the frontier and free land. With the closing of the frontier, the exhaustion of free land, the growth of population, and the coming of large-scale production, the basis of ownership was transformed. If property rights are to be diffused in industrial society, natural resources and all important forms of capital will have to be collectively owned. Obviously every citizen cannot hold title to a mine, a factory, a railroad, a department store, or even a thoroughly mechanized farm. This clearly means that, if democracy is to survive in the United States, it must abandon its individualistic affiliations in the sphere of economics. What precise form a democratic society will take in the age of science and the machine, we cannot know with any assurance today. We must, however, insist on two things: first, that technology be released from the fetters and the domination of every type of special privilege; and, second, that the resulting system of production and distribution be made to serve directly the masses of the people. Within these limits, as I see it, our democratic tradition must of necessity evolve and gradually

assume an essentially collectivistic pattern. The only conceivable alternative is the abandonment of the last vestige of democracy and the frank adoption of some modern form of feudalism.

5

THE IMPORTANT POINT is that fundamental changes in the economic system are imperative. Whatever services historic capitalism may have rendered in the past, and they have been many, its days are numbered. With its deification of the principle of selfishness, its exaltation of the profit motive, its reliance upon the forces of competition, and its placing of property above human rights, it will either have to be displaced altogether or changed so radically in form and spirit that its identity will be completely lost. In view of the fact that the urge for private gain tends to debase everything that it touches, whether business, recreation, religion, art, or friendship, the indictment against capitalism has commonly been made on moral grounds. But today the indictment can be drawn in other terms.

Capitalism is proving itself weak at the very point where its champions have thought it impregnable. It is failing to meet the pragmatic test; it no longer works; it is unable even to organize and maintain production. In its present form capitalism is not only cruel and inhuman; it is also wasteful and inefficient. It has exploited our

natural resources without the slightest regard for the future needs of our society; it has forced technology to serve the interests of the few rather than the many; it has chained the engineer to the vagaries and inequities of the price system; it has plunged the great nations of the earth into a succession of wars ever more devastating and catastrophic in character; and only recently it has brought on a world crisis of such dimensions that the entire economic order is paralyzed and millions of men in all the great industrial countries are deprived of the means of livelihood. The growth of science and technology has carried us into a new age where ignorance must be replaced by knowledge, competition by cooperation, trust in providence by careful planning, and private capitalism by some form of socialized economy.

Already the individualism of the pioneer and the farmer, produced by free land, great distances, economic independence, and a largely self-sustaining family economy, is without solid foundation in either agriculture or industry. Free land has long since disappeared. Great distances have been shortened immeasurably by invention. Economic independence survives only in the traditions of our people. Self-sustaining family economy has been swallowed up in a vast society which even refuses to halt before the boundaries of nations. Already we live in an economy which in its functions is fundamentally cooperative.

There remains the task of reconstructing our economic institutions and of reformulating our social ideals so that they may be in harmony with the underlying facts of life. The man who would live unto himself alone must retire from the modern world. The day of individualism in the production and distribution of goods is gone. The fact cannot be overemphasized that choice is no longer between individualism and collectivism. It is rather between two forms of collectivism: the one essentially democratic, the other feudal in spirit; the one devoted to the interests of the people, the other to the interests of a privileged class.

The objection is of course raised at once that a planned, coordinated, and socialized economy, managed in the interests of the people, would involve severe restrictions on personal freedom. Undoubtedly in such an economy the individual would not be permitted to do many things that he has customarily done in the past. He would not be permitted to carve a fortune out of the natural resources of the nation, to organize a business purely for the purpose of making money, to build a new factory or railroad whenever and wherever he pleased, to throw the economic system out of gear for the protection of his own private interests, to amass or to attempt to amass great riches by the corruption of the political life, the control of the organs of opinion, the manipulation of the financial machinery, the purchase of brains and knowledge, or the exploitation of ignorance, frailty, and misfortune. In exchange for such privileges as these, which only the few could ever enjoy, we would secure the complete and uninterrupted functioning of the productive system and thus lay the foundations for a measure of freedom for the many that mankind has never known in the past. Freedom without a secure economic foundation is only a word: in our society it may be freedom to beg, steal, or starve. The right to vote, if it cannot be made to insure the right to work, is but an empty bauble. Indeed it may be less than a bauble: it may serve to drug and dull the senses of the masses. Today only the members of the plutocracy are really free, and even in their case freedom is rather precarious. If all of us could be assured of material security and abundance, we would be released from economic worries and our energies liberated to grapple with the central problems of cultural advance.

Under existing conditions, however, no champion of the democratic way of life can view the future with equanimity. If democracy is to be achieved in the industrial age, powerful classes must be persuaded to surrender their privileges, and institutions deeply rooted in popular prejudice will have to be radically modified or abolished. And according to the historical record, this process has commonly been attended by bitter struggle and even bloodshed. Ruling classes never surrender their privileges voluntarily. Rather do they cling to what they have been accustomed to regard as their rights, even though the heavens fall. Men customarily defend their property, however it may have been acquired, as tenaciously as the proverbial mother defends her young. There is little evidence from the pages of American history to support us in the hope that we may adjust our difficulties through the method of sweetness and light. Since the settlement of the first colonists along the Atlantic seaboard we have practiced and become inured to violence. This is peculiarly true wherever and whenever property rights, actual or potential, have been involved. Consider the pitiless extermination of the Indian tribes and the internecine strife over the issue of human slavery. Consider the long reign of violence in industry, from the days of the Molly Maguires in the seventies down to the strikes in the mining regions of Kentucky today. Also let those, whose memories reach back a dozen years, recall the ruthlessness with which the privileged classes put down every expression of economic or political dissent during the period immediately following the World War. When property is threatened, constitutional guarantees are but scraps of paper and even the courts and the churches, with occasional exceptions, rush to the support of privilege and vested interest.

This is a dark picture. If we look at the future through the eyes of the past, we find little reason for optimism. If there is to be no break in our tradition of violence, if a bold and realistic program of education is not forthcoming, we can only anticipate a struggle of increasing bitterness terminating in revolution and disaster. And yet, as regards the question of property, the present situation has no historical parallel. In earlier paragraphs I have pointed to the possibility of completely disposing of the economic problem. For the first time in history we are able to produce all the goods and services that our people can consume. The justification, or at least the rational basis, of the age-long struggle for property has been removed. This situation gives to teachers an opportunity and a responsibility unique in the annals of education.

In an economy of scarcity, where the population always tends to outstrip the food supply, any attempt to change radically the rules of the game must inevitably lead to trial by the sword. But in an economy of plenty, which the growth of technology has made entirely possible, the conditions are fundamentally altered. It is natural and understandable for men to fight when there is scarcity, whether it be over air, water, food, or women. For them to fight over the material goods of life in America today is sheer insanity. Through the courageous and intelligent reconstruction of their economic institutions they could all obtain, not only physical security, but also the luxuries of life and as much leisure as men could ever learn to enjoy. For those who take delight in combat, ample provision for strife could of course be made; but the more cruel aspects of the human struggle would be considerably softened. As the possibilities in our society begin to dawn upon us, we are all, I think, growing increasingly weary of the brutalities, the stupidities, the hypocrisies, and the gross inanities of contemporary life. We have a haunting feeling that we were born for better things and that the nation itself is falling far short of its powers. The fact that other groups refuse to deal boldly and realistically with the present situation does not justify the teachers of the country in their customary policy of hesitation and equivocation. The times are literally crying for a new vision of American destiny. The teaching profession, or at least its progressive elements, should eagerly grasp the opportunity which the fates have placed in their hands.

Such a vision of what America might become in the industrial age I would introduce into our schools as the supreme imposition, but one to which our children are entitled—a priceless legacy which it should be the first concern of our profession to fashion and bequeath. The objection will of course be raised that this is asking teachers to assume unprecedented social responsibilities. But we live in difficult and dangerous times—times when precedents lose their significance. If we are content to remain where all is safe and quiet and serene, we shall dedicate ourselves, as teachers have commonly done in the past, to a role of futility, if not of positive social reaction. Neutrality with respect to the great issues that agitate society, while perhaps theoretically possible, is practically tantamount to giving support to the forces of conservatism. As Justice Holmes has candidly said in his essay on Natural Law, "we all, whether we know it or not, are fighting to make the kind of world that we should like." If neutrality is impossible even in the dispensation of justice, whose emblem is the blindfolded goddess, how is it to be achieved in education? To ask the question is to answer it.

To refuse to face the task of creating a vision of a future America immeasurably more just and noble and beautiful than the America of today is to evade the most crucial, difficult, and important educational task. Until we have assumed this responsibility we are scarcely justified in opposing and mocking the efforts of so-called patriotic societies to introduce into the schools a tradition which, though narrow and unenlightened, nevertheless represents an honest attempt to meet a profound social and educational need. Only when we have fashioned a finer and more authentic vision than they will we be fully justified in our opposition to their efforts. Only then will we have discharged the age-long obligation which the older generation owes to the younger and which no amount of sophistry can obscure. Only through such a legacy of spiritual values will our children be enabled to find their place in the world, be lifted out of the present morass of moral indifference, be liberated from the senseless struggle for material success, and be challenged to high endeavor and achievement. And only thus will we as a people put ourselves on the road to the expression of our peculiar genius and to the making of our special contribution to the cultural heritage of the race.

A Note on the Text

THE TEXT of this book combines three papers
that George Counts read at national educational
meetings in February of 1932; the papers were
"Dare Progressive Education Be Progressive," to
the Progressive Education Association; "Education through Indoctrination," to a division of the
Department of Superintendence; and "Freedom,
Culture, Social Planning, and Leadership," to the
National Council of Education.

First published as a book by the John Day
Company in 1932, this work was reprinted numerous times from the original plates. By 1969
it had long been out of print when the Arno Press
and The New York Times published a limited
facsimile edition of one hundred copies in the
series American Education: Its Men, Ideas and
Institutions.

The complete text has been newly set in type
for the present edition with no editorial intervention save in mechanical matters.

Jo Ann Boydston